AF334831

Space/Gap/Interval/Distance

Space/Gap/Interval/Distance

Judy Halebsky

Sixteen Rivers Press

Thanks to the editors of the following journals for including my
work: *Hotel Amerika*: "talent child many illness" and *"negaeri"*;
Joy + Ride: "Learning to Dance"; *Ping-Pong*: "Transmission" and
"A Breaking Word"; *Poetry Kanto*: "Space/Gap/Interval/Distance,"
"A thread for a nest, a word for a vein," "Rad. 122," and "Rad. 84";
Sow's Ear: "Dig Me Up at the Riverbed"; *Squaw Valley Review*:
"Stopping Between Butter and Whipped Cream."
Thanks also to the MacDowell Colony, the Millay Colony,
the Squaw Valley Community of Writers, the Headlands Center
for the Arts, the Japanese Ministry of Culture,
the Ohno Studio, the Sacramento Poets, Yuka Tsukagoshi,
and everyone at Sixteen Rivers Press.

Published by Sixteen Rivers Press
P.O. Box 640663
San Francisco, CA 94164
www.sixteenrivers.org

Library of Congress Catalog Card Number: 2011938809
ISBN: 978-0-9819816-5-9

Cover art: *Utterance Upon Utterance*, by Jennifer Kaufman
Design: Carolyn Miller

*In memory of butoh dancer and teacher Kazuo Ohno
(1906–2010)*

Contents

From the darkness and the fireflies, he calls me
mapless, unguided, night walker

pulling night from clear blue day to that heavy blue
when there's still a little light in the sky
and the trees are dark against it

I am hiding in those trees
on a branch in the sway with the wind
not holding on so much as balancing
he calls me the night traveler
the angel breather
he calls me the one who has not come home

A THREAD FOR A NEST, A WORD FOR A VEIN

She is sending cupcakes out the window
in a basket tied with string

Frida stacking flowers in her hair

Aunt Nina scrubbing blouses back to white

Emily sending poems out in letters
in the needle hem of a dress

she is trading pinecones for cookies
feathers for scones

彫　　　心　　　鏤　　骨
carve　　heart　　set　　bone:
carefully　polishing　　a　　poem

it was later when all she could muster
was to sit at the top of the stairs
while her sister played piano below

it was after her nephew died
so many bottles into the sea

I have followed nights in moss
on the north side of trees

LEARNING TO DANCE

(Kazuo Ohno Studio, April 2008)

The Italian had on silver high heels
her hair tied in seashells
while Sensei talked she whispered me the important parts

I am an old man carrying a dozen apples

I am walking through the train station struck by lightning

grass has light
milk has cream
these are things I need to remember:
              foil-wrap wings
              birds with fragile beaks
              the angle of the earth to the sun

      these are the primary colors: plum, pine, bamboo
                  liquor, denim, daybreak

the Italian
(plum blossoms finally in April)
she says,
    I was like, beautiful
putting in what was missing
the high heels, the apples
I was like to mean *the whole of me*

Space/Gap/Interval/Distance

I.
I have spent too many days counting
butter or cream cheese
4 or 6 or 8
how to piece in the hours like a layer cake

Lorca and your olive fields
Ginsberg and your mountain dream
I have been a paper doll
not thinking of the rain

間 *ma*

written as the sun
coming through the gate

as what we leave open
between us
so the spirits   when they come
will have a place to land

II.

The day we drove from the coast back to Sacramento
the sun fell in broad strokes as we leaned into the curve
you were looking at me and I caught your eyes

wish I could have known it then
to mark that feeling in ink
as a stamp
a letter
something I could send in the mail
that would come out of the envelope
just as it had gone in—

carefully written
bled into
and only half-parted with

Stopping Between Whipped Cream and Butter

Abby at eleven is taller than me, rounder than me
has more freckles and knows everything

she can tell the difference between 20 and 21
21-year-olds are cranky
she says and puckers up her face

pine trees live for hundreds of years
so they carry more scars

> *a confession*
> *an orchid*
> *a baby gorilla*

pine: to waste away through grief

birch: a tree with paper-thin bark

when I go home Warren says *you have a wicked bad
American accent*

there are all kinds of ways to fail

> *a piecrust*
> *a snowflake*

spring melt   June thaw
how to unbend   unscar

the birch tree
slightly wounded
is growing toward the sun

WALK THE LINE

Bend the spine of a thesaurus—
my shadow map, guide of distances
atlas of cities

if this book were a bridge I would trust my weight to it

late bloomer, mountain azalea, dwarf pine

the letters didn't always make words
there were years and years
when they just stayed letters

I have come to feel the moss under the water
I have come to put my feet in the creek

Basho and Sora on pilgrimage
write on their hats:
no home in heaven or earth
on this path we go two together

(monks on pilgrimage, *by two we go*
the monk alone but with the dharma
Basho alone but with Sora
me and the library with 20,000 other fools
and a mother who wants a postcard

a line on a Christmas note
a baby girl to walk
a two-wheel bicycle, a spelling bee
a pirouette, a finger to trace the letters across the page
the letters to make a song)

some say they fought
some say they parted in anger

after Sora stayed behind
Basho let the words *by two we go*
wash off his hat in the rain

at graduation, my mother, hands in the air
shouts *it's a miracle, a miracle*

才子多病
talent child many illness:
whom gods love die young

Out of the Gate

I have breathed into a thousand balloons

put my fingers in so many cakes

had my body scanned with fingerprints

wrote out my dreams in lines of the night

traced words into storm clouds

mixed water with mint and bourbon

made a bed of spidering vines

wore a wreath of grass cuttings

a raft of stickseed

there's a snail who thinks he's climbing Mount Fuji

the racetrack is filled with stars

RAD. 网 122

Amigashira: *crown. Variant: net shaped like eye.*

I ask Joey how far the human eye can see
he wants to say forever
but he says, *you can see stars, right?*

I know then that he will never leave me

買   net over a clam shell: to buy

貝   clam shell for money

目   eye for eye

gambling is for when there aren't other options

how far I can see into the distance
depends on the light, not my eyes

Snapshots

Standing shoulder to shoulder on the train
we count the years between us

are you married, she asks
and smiles this would-I, could-I
shake-your-head, fifty-years-ago smile

save a square of cardboard under the tree for rain

紅 葉
fall leaves:
small hands
hands like fall leaves

I stitch a quarter into the hem of my skirt

close to shore
there's a place where the waves
are going in and out at the same time

言 葉
speaking leaves:
a language

which means standing still

you're not married, she asks again

to hold down in the wind
for an ice cream, a phone call

I stitch a quarter in the hem of my skirt

Dig Me Up at the Riverbed

I.
Dig me up at the riverbed
knead the air out of me
shake me down
reclaim me
from failed tea bowls
from would-have-been handles, saucers, spouts

I can take a thumbprint
I can hold the shape of your palm
the spines of a leaf, a chestnut, newspaper ash

porcelain is a certain kind of clay
luminous but fragile
weak to gravity, to other plates

mix me down with shale
with a sturdy field crystal
mix me
down
so I'll hold at the waist
so you can throw me thin
so the light will pass through us

II.
No one likes plates, he says
they take up too much space in the kiln

to fire porcelain, we'll mix it with paper
we'll pile in wood up to 1200 degrees

I can't believe how long we've been together, he says
as if we're at the beach in a patch of sun

a wedding band, an Allen key, a dress too tight

we need air and water constantly

closed with a brick
there's a tiny window into the kiln

don't look, he says
wear a glove to move the brick

no one likes plates, he says
they break too easily

I can't believe how long we've been together, I say
as if it's been raining for days

don't look, he says
hold your hand near it to feel the heat

III.
Lay your snail spine as a mold for me
make your room into a leaf house
an umbrella in the rain house
bed of moss
palm cup
clay doorstep
telephone lines into vines
we, who are not yet kiln fired
we, who might vanish in the heat

ALONG THE WAY

世に降るも更にそうぎの宿りかな
In this world, our life passes, temporary shelter

—Basho

To make his life bigger than the corners of a desk
bigger than 18 scoops of ice cream
a four-lane highway, a 747
he wants to get married

    Christmas cake: to get old quickly
    evening wedding: in the nick of time

a poet friend advises Basho to live within his means

    spinning maid, sitting maid, window watcher

first the house, then plates and chairs
butter knives, serving spoons

    our life, in this world, passing/falling, a temporary shelter

(the verb for getting old also means falling, the way rain falls)

a bride in the last flourish of her youth: evening wedding
a girl, good until her twenty-fifth: Christmas cake

pass over: to be left behind
pass over: to escape

our life falling the way rain falls

this world, a brief shelter

a newspaper hat in the rain

There are ways that I am watering
the same tree for hours

what if it comes out
we were never in love

the reach of the branches
marks the span of the roots

I water to the edge of the canopy

there are things that can't sustain being looked at directly

water does not travel sideways

the biggest risk is what we lose to the atmosphere

寝返り
negaeri

turning over while sleeping:
betrayal

別

betsu

branch off, diverge, scatter

Maiden, spinster, night lover
the one who lives alone

by alone, I mean leaving
I mean there are many ways to be blind
I mean ocean
I mean airplane
I mean fathom, glacier, marathon, hectare

months ago in late-April sun
I learned the path to your studio
melting the edges of pine-shaded snow

pipe smoker, winemaker, waterer of moss
your beard scratching my shoulder
our shape in the window
half-hidden by leaves

verdant is a word for this kind of green

there are bird sounds in the train station
so you can walk with your eyes closed

betsu: separate
used here as goodbye

the sun is burning your outline across the field
straw yellow to ash
I hold my hand up to the glare

betsu: to break, to scatter, to fly

Garden Trees

Bent for elegance
shaped for wingspan
grown into the broadest spread of pine needles and leaves

ankle-tie heels, charcoal eyeliner, a strapless dress

stretching out the branches weakens them

to stay upright
we bend at the knees
dance with both feet on the floor
weight ourselves against gravity

it's not polite to walk where the neighbors hang their clothes

don't ask for a story you already know

my sister says, *move to Vancouver*
so when Daddy can't see, you can hold his arm

Daddy says, *she went to the best schools, the best*

weakened to things that fall: rain, baby birds, piecrusts
spatulas, feathers, bridges, volcanic ash, broken kites

prop up the branches to carry the weight
in case of lightning or electric love
in case one person looks away

we hide from things that fall

freezing rain, pinecones, confetti
the branches of other trees

RAD. 气 84

Kigame: "vapor" enclosure. Nickname: steam.

气   *ki*: spirit, air, taste, touch, shade, trace

air divided = mood

taste color = to look hurt

feeling feeling = to always worry

to feel up = students influenced by communism

feeling already = spirits of the dead

my father is calling to me from both sides of the grave, holding his thick dense body up by the railing, in the mist off English Bay, he wants to bring me with him, to circulate my blood, he wants to be someone else, younger, himself fifty years ago, when it was clear that, yes, City College will strike, the union is strong, he says bagel, he says yogurt, he says there's three boats in the harbor and just one will carry him away

A Breaking Word

There's that part
after Basho writes
old still pond
of pressing a fingerprint into wet clay

where the word *ya*
holds a space in the air
a cloud changes shape in the sky

make it a dash, a murmur
a breath on the inhale

this old pond
so many have tried to open

a sigh, a hum, a—

frog jumps in

sound of water says Hass
plop says Watts
kerplunk says Ginsberg

The Ohno Studio

I.
When he couldn't walk
he would sit
and dance
with his hands
dashing like birds

now at over a hundred
he is sleeping in the house next door
we take off our shoes and stretch
his son writes the characters:

雪　　snow

花　　flower

月　　moon

some die like snow, he says
it's beautiful at dusk
and then the next day
where's the snow

or a flower
blooming all in one season

or the moon, little by little
waning

II.
After floating his hands in the air above his head
angling them out in raw jagged lines
balls of raw silk
a snail in a shell
he started to cry
not a little bit but tears streaking down his cheeks

window frames, rooftops, fences and fields, bony hips knobby
knees, the dancing Antonia Mercé, I have torn off all the layers,
I have looked straight into the darkness, I have called spirits of
the dead, I have let them take my voice, take my body, I have
brought back what I have lost and danced here with them, my
mother, my sister, the years hungry and burned

one girl said he's crying because he can't talk
another offered he's crying because he can't dance

in this studio
I have laid down my fears
I have been easily hurt
snow melts, flowers bloom
there is getting up off the floor
the third pine
the ground, the sky, the space between
this is where I have danced
this is where I leave you from

Growing up on the east coast of Canada, I walked each morning through a gate into a French-speaking world of playgrounds and classrooms. At 3:15 P.M., I crossed back into the English-speaking world of the bus and my neighborhood. Years later, when I came to study Japanese as a adult, I carried with me that experience of moving between languages and trying to piece them together. Learning Japanese offered a shifting kaleidoscope of ways to make meaning and sound. It gave me new conceptions of words that dovetailed with the work of making poems.

The Kazuo Ohno Studio, in Yokohama, Japan, sits at the top of a long, winding street. Entering the studio for butoh dance classes was again a movement between languages, this time from spoken language to a language of dance that seeks to reject the rules of language, grammar, and the confines of established form. In a way, butoh also seeks to reject social time and the separation between the worlds of the living and the dead.

The poems in this collection come out of a process of making meaning across languages, trying to account for the uneven shifting and the continual failing to find an equivalency. Nelson's *Japanese-English Character Dictionary* became a source for material that I employed selectively and combined with multiple other sources in making poems. Following are notes to a few sources that shaped these poems. The haiku translations are my own.

Page 4: "Space/Gap/Interval/Distance" incorporates the aesthetic concept of *ma,* which refers to the space between actions, events, or objects. *Ma* is used to describe timing in music as well as a sensitivity to space and intensity in dance, acting, and other art forms.

Ma is written as 間, by combining the character 門 ("gate") and 日 ("sun"). The Japanese kanji character thus communicates the concept of *ma* through the image of sunlight coming through a gate.

Page 8: "Walk the Line" draws on Basho's haiku:

今日よりや書き付け消さん笠の露

from today the writing extinguished from my hat by dew

Page 11: "Out of the Gate" alludes to Issa's haiku:

かたつぶりそろそろ登れ富士の山

a snail, little by little, climbing Mount Fuji

Pages 12 and 26: "Rad. 122" and "Rad. 84", draw on the layout and translations found in Andrew Nelson's *Japanese-English Character Dictionary* (Tokyo: Charles E. Tuttle Company, 1974). The dictionary is arranged not in alphabetical order but by the number of strokes required to write the 214 radical characters. Radicals are the root characters that generally form words on their own and are also the basic units of more complex characters. In these poems, *Rad.* is an abbreviation of *Radical.*

Page 27: "A Breaking Word" draws on Basho's most famous haiku and translations of that haiku by Robert Hass, Alan Watts, and Allen Ginsberg.

古池や蛙飛び込む水の音

old pond, a frog jumps in, sound of water

Kazuo Ohno and Hijikata Tatsumi originated butoh dance in Japan's post-war era. *Butoh* is short for *ankoku butō*, which has been translated by Susan Blakeley Klein, a professor of Japanese literature, as "the dance of utter darkness." It is a dance form that rejects established dance traditions and searches for untrained movements of the body. Kazuo Ohno died in 2010 at the age of 103. Under the leadership of his son Yoshito, the Ohno studio continues to be an international center for butoh dance.

About the Author

Judy Halebsky's book *Sky = Empty*, won the New Issues
Poetry Prize and was a finalist for the California Book Award.
The MacDowell Colony, the Millay Colony, and the Canada
Council for the Arts have supported her work. Born and raised in
Nova Scotia, Canada, she studied art and literature in Japan for five
years on fellowships from the Japanese Ministry of Culture.
With a collective of Tokyo poets, she edits and translates the
bilingual poetry journal *Eki Mae*. She lives in San Francisco and
teaches at Dominican University of California.

Display type: BlairMdlTC TT Medium

Text type: Garamond

Kanji characters: Hiragino Micho Pro

Printed in Canada by Hignell Book Printing on recycled paper